The   Makeup

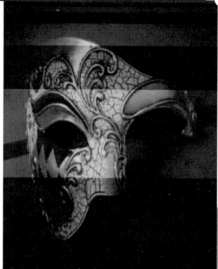

Everybody paints their face...

By: Chris Grace

CHRIS GRACE

By: Chris Grace

2/19/2020

Day Dreaming

I'm daydreaming a perfect vision. Knowing the pain and sorrow of tomorrow still I took the mission.

A little stressed but, I stayed persistent. A lot of tears, a lot of laughs, a lot of fights but don't get it twisted.

Every moment was another step. Every job was another test, every kiss was another breath

No more days of waking up in cold sweats because I fly, I grew my wings when I stuck out my chest.

I knew something about loyalty and love and respect. So, as my world was falling down, I only progressed...

Or should I say when things didn't go my way; I never left something was always telling me to stay.

I've always found the door, leading to another way...

I've always found the bottom useful just to give me strength. I took advantage of all that I could grasp. Because all I had was all I knew I needed for the task.

Daily installing in my head, built to last! My next move I made it clear but never put on blast...

Quiet as kept but silence is death. Experience is knowledge gained and that's why I'm blessed...

A Hidden Message

There are some who will reap... There are others who will sow.
In those times we are together. One truth is to be told...

You can run, you could hide. Slow down, or fast. You can
pray but don't say the real message was never passed...

Have you taken a double look when you opened
a book? Felt hopeless or felt ashamed...

Flip it maybe you've even gained... You still
can't escape this well-known truth. Everything
that you see ultimately reflects you.

Whether ugly, pretty, or a beautiful disaster. Your life
is like a book, can you see your next chapter?

A miss-understanding; the wrong interpretation, or a distorted
perception will always lead you to a road you may not have
intentionally intended to be on. You attract things that you
may have felt the need to avoid. At the same time! You manifest
every desire you were consciously predestined to have...
Life is about choices. Your emotions and your subconscious

thoughts are very vital. Even essential to every decision we make. Though unexpected, we ultimately realize that we can't fight fate. What's yours will always be. If you do not have it now, it will find its way through you... What isn't meant for you will never be in your grasp, it easily slips away. How can the world be yours if you didn't make it? Can we truly predict and take control of our futures? Do we really know our history? Have we ever really escaped from our past? These are all questions I find it foolish not to ask...

Change

How do you get someone to see, that their definition
of strong is weak...?

How do you let someone know... Problems seem big
when faith is small but minimize as it grows?

What do you tell a person when they ask how...? How
can I reach the top by being turned upside down...?

Better yet, what does it really take to win people over...?

Genuine acts of love...

Over and over...!

Efficient in Black

There were many days I felt alive I said. The times
you're happy just to open your eyes I said!

Arise and display it. The greatness that's inside don't betray it...
For all the nights I shed tears the perfect time to convey it...

Seek every opportunity and you'll find the map.

Dark and cold, night or day stay efficient in black. Keep your
distance from the traps. Stay consistent and in fact...

Stay persistent hope replaces every limit that you lack.
You envisioned it; a dream is just a thought on a plaque.

I hustled my whole life, I envision success. Couldn't see
it being handed to me, Santa was standing through me!
Planted in a jacuzzi with animals running loosely...

Shooting more than a movie this may sound a little
spooky. But you must listen!

Trust is given & earned. Money's a must & a privilege...
Stick to the guns & butter! Love's a lust in a village...

Trust your decisions. Your faith will be the thrust
to some endless... Hopes and wishes. Unless of
course you want something different...

Even if it came all the hunger from your pain
might just change your perspective...

Humbled about some things. Ready to rumble
about some change!

I swear if it's not in you, you'll just stumble into shame...

The One who knows your name knows who's meant for the fame. Or who might abuse it. No choosing differences get exchanged; every gift is not the same. Do with yours as you will but leave mines where it is at. It's there for a reason.

Ever wonder why the sun was pitched in black...? Ever wonder why you wonder, about the lightning and the thunder?

Storms will make you feel under while a spark shifts you back... It's just a different impact. Whether it tickles or smacks!

That's why I say to every race stay efficient in black...

Fear

Why do I let my fears consume me? What traumatizes
my mind so deep that I allow my fears to ruin me?
Rob me of everything I know that I'm worth...

Love, happiness and peace. The greatest gifts on this earth.
Fears take control of thoughts and make you lose all purpose.
Feeling hopeless and helpless. Lonely and undeserving...
Fear tells you what you can't do even if you say I can. Fear
tells you your inferior until you say I am! Fear can have
you feeling worthless emotions hit rock bottom. The
graveyard or jail cell doesn't seem like a problem...

Open My Eyes

Open my eyes, allow me to see through the shade....

Open my mind, enlighten me humble my ways...

Strengthen my heart!!!

The strong survive but my demons they still arise...

I'm not surprised what goes around comes back...

Can't expect to live in peace with a heart so black...

But keep pumping! Tell heaven we are coming
we're already in hell...

These ashes are worth something!

Seeds of A Goldmine

Salute the real winners...

It's hard to deal with us, but it's a spade every time...

The memories from when we unwind...

You wish we would change though we tried...

Consistent same lane we reside...

The stain never dries...

The pain be so alive couldn't miss it even if we road by...

To twist it you should ask yourself why...

Diamonds in the rough; that's a seed of a goldmine...

We aim high though considered as a low life!

Running from Love

I'm good with the word play. Like foreplay your nerves play.
I send chills up your spine and vibrate your vertebrae.

Your mind is saying something's special about this person
truthfully. I don't feel the empty words people say to me usually.

I just speak the truth any language I speak fluently. I advanced
my relationship skills. Communicating beautifully.

Have you thinking, is this all real, or too good to be true?
Think all you want but wasting time's a bad habit. When
opportunity presents itself it's best to take advantage.
Hold on to the truth, let your heart be the judge… If it's
all good, then why are you running from love?

The Flower that blooms in Adversity
Is the most Rare and Beautiful of
All. (Disney, Mulan, 1998)

Inseparable

I wish that I could see you.

I know I feel your presence.

I know you're still here.

But I just can't accept it!

The fact that you are gone.

With you I felt so protected.

Now my heart is almost empty.

I'm hurt deep on the inside.

I remember the love you gave.

I haven't found it since so I...

Kind of feel lost.

My emotions always toss and turns.

Serenity is truly what my heart yearns for.

But everyday I live, I learn more.

The problems that I face.

Keeps me concerned more.

Then I hunger for you.

I read the scriptures and I wonder.

Are they honestly true!

I realized faith is hope in a belief; even when I see no proof...

I exercise it all the time in everything that I do.

Even this message to you!

I'm learning how to discern more.

Separate what's real from how I feel.

When I'm stressed or things don't go how I expect.

It takes a minute...

In the end I finally see I'm blessed.

I humble myself, every day I rumble myself!

I persevere in spite all my fears.

Still I'm hold back tears.

Just wishing that you were here.

But I keep you in my thoughts, in my spirit and my heart.

Gone but never forgotten...

Nothing could tear us apart...

Because even if it did... I'm still standing strong. I can't be moved! Winning is on my mind I refuse to lose. How can I lose hope? Love will always leverage all faith...

So, while you're in my heart I will always see your face.

Inseparable, life or death...

Stamped

The snakes are no longer in the grass...

They are in your future.

They are in your past, and present.

In your trash and your blessings!

Relaxed and aggressive.

Manifested in your essence to exit.

Life is a lesson...

Yeah, we all have been tested.

I suggest you understand like perspective...

When you finally find the answer just know it is best to keep it protected!

Stamped and tattooed stay glued to your buried treasure.

Your deepest core should stay concealed no pressure...

Only reveal when it's time to kill!

With not intent to cause hell but to show the world that Heaven is real.

I wish you well!

I know the devil's about to send its appeal.

If it's approved

Understand, God gave all free will.

We choose the gun, but do we heal?

No, the shooter dies.

The victim was a shield from the pain that we feel.

Stamped in blood is a love too real!

Many searched but few find.

That's how it is until the end of time.

It always was and remains, balance is key to change.

The time is now if you really wish to break every chain...

"If my thoughts riddle you maybe, I'll speak more clearly. To the one who here's me. Or even noticed my voice. We're set a part for a reason... Part of it is by choice. The only part I play is making a choice to be a voice. Shed some words and give insight from my reality of course. Nothing I've ever felt was forced; persuaded at most. For most of my hopes and wishes I risked jail and approached... A kitchen hell had provoked but I excelled through the smoke. My definition of hustle: Either sail or stay afloat. Many try to fight gravity me I try to get close. Certain things can't be explained but it's a reason it happened. The main lesson of it all is who and what gets impacted..."

Keep Moving Forward

Never find it strange…

When people, places, or things are starting to change.

Progression is a process.

It involves being rearranged…

So, readjust! However, wherever and whenever stepping up is necessary…

Keep in mind that the struggle builds the muscle.

Also, we all are driven by our own passions.

Whether a dream, or a burning desire…

Stay aware and conscious of the areas you may lack in.

Giving up leaves me nowhere. It left me stuck.

Because if you're not moving forward, you'll start backing up.

There is no between.

Every successful person in this world is still chasing a dream…

It makes since just looking at the facts.

You get a taste of true happiness; you want nothing less than that.

A Limitless Dove

Acting like she worthless.

I see her worth more now that I'm peeking through the surface.

Pureness of a virgin...

Assurance that's for certain!

It's a must I keep insurance just for hurting.

My plans are unpredictable when working.

My demands don't always come out nursing.

But when in need of a doctor I take initiative to come out urgent.

Not always prepared...

But I see the thrill of a surgent!

As humble as servants

Precisely like a marvelous serpent.

Ouroboros lurking!

Searching for a love that's deserving.

I trust that I'm worthy, my love is clean my lust keeps me dirty.

My word is bond, my scars are deep, but my future is bright.

My pain is purpose, passion, predestined and pleasing some nights...

I may have felt low at times, but I connected to above.

In visions of love soaring like a limitless dove...

It's often said that love is blind… In my humblest answer based on my own hypothesis from my own personal experience I'd say… We as people are highly attracted to a mere image that only exists in our own minds. Rather than taking the time to recognize a very noticeable reality. Because normally it contradicts with certain relations, we are more familiar with. You'll hear things like, "people love different." Or "My world is different from yours." Either statement is very much true to a certain degree… It's human nature to rationalize or try to make things make sense especially when they're mind bottling… You say tomato I say tom`ato. You say potato I say pot`ato… At some point in time you must ask yourself is it really that big of a deal? Does the difference make that much of a difference? Correct me if I'm wrong. Even when it comes to math or even science. Certain problems can be solved in various ways but, there's only one right answer… Whether we accept it or not!

Sweet Sugar and Spice...
Everything You Like...

I face more devils than a little.

More fettle for the fickle...

A dash of your time...

A beauty mark that won't belittle!

Swivel and swerve you deserve more...

Time will tell...

I set a spell just to see you prevail.

Never fail, but don't tell keep a secret Miguel...

Keep the truth in your right hand just to sweep up the L's.

In due time you'll reach your peak.

Leap and tip all the scales...

You will get it right one day, I can already tell...

With sweet sugar and spice...

Everything seems nice...

Life is a little less bland...

Though it was not as you planned.

The taste of fate shouldn't tangle you.

We were born to expand...

So, I'll give you the best of both worlds
since that's what you demand.

*"Your eyes see what your heart feels...
It's pricey but the thought's real."*

*Life is about taking chances. Always
strive for what you believe in. Do
what you must to Achieve It...*

Let It Flow Away

Water...

For your eyes to see. What your ears don't hear.

When your mind won't speak...

Because your heart will feel, what your soul won't teach...

So, through the fire we breeze, at our boldest peak.

Let me roll in peace...'

Let me rest my case...

Faith will tell you to leap!

Fear will press you to stay!

Hope will push you to love...

Envy will drive you to hate...

Remember humble beginnings!

Try to balance your pace...

Flesh of my flesh...!

Bread of my life!

Bodies of living water...

Keep me, cleanse me right.

Dilate this olive oil used to stain my life.

Lubricate every vessel...

Loose every chain on my life.

Before we all say cheers, I just want to say…

Traditions and limitations can now flow away…

"Everything isn't meant to go with you to your next level. Everybody isn't meant to come either. Ash to ash dust to dust. Keep in mind we only live once."

Make It Personal

When I think about success... It's personal to me! A cherished view I see... Living all I've dreamed. One day you will see...

It's the reason my heart beats... When they quit, I proceed!

Driven by my beliefs, because hope is all I need! The roadblocks in between... I used to strengthen me!

Because it's personal to me...

When I'm chained, I will break free. I find a crack in every wall that I see! I find purpose for my adversity.

I let nothing ever come in between. This cherished view I see. Because it's personal to me...!

The Main Attraction

You'd be surprised by what you attract!

Some may find you amusing, others may feel relaxed.

It really isn't your place to orchestrate all the facts.

Just let your music be heard, and copyright every track!

Destiny is an art that's displayed in war! Win or lose
any battle, the fight is what we endure...

I'd rather my past pull up than my future pressing down. You
can see from different angles only one vision is profound!

Survival of the fittest but to fit it is a style...

Enlightened so all critics either whistle or go Wow...

Be Ready

Why don't you just follow instructions...

All this corruption and still no justice!

They want to take you out...

They try to keep you sleep!

They want to know, no matter what it takes to keep you weak...

The meek shall inherit the Earth... Though you must find that underground railroad to really see what it's worth!

Get a little grimy ironically, you'll uplift her skirts.

The innocent gets arrested and placed on enemy turf! They acknowledge your presence. But our they pay pennies to flirt!

Over-look your intelligence offering meaningless work.

Be skeptical of this development you see being birthed.

Take precaution; you know often it's a dream at first...

Then you notice deleted scenes, the bigger picture gets worse...

Hard to fathom being deceived but as they say the truth hurts!

Why Should I Sleep at A Time Like This?

Why should I sleep at a time like this...?

All the storms in my life; it's a battle to make it through the night.

I know hard times don't last forever but, instead
of waiting for it to pass...

I meditate on what I can grasp to rise above this storm
of life and reach a height that I never have...

Because if nothing changes nothing changes...

How will I ever see better days if in my mind I'm always
complaining?

Although it's dark I refuse to sleep; I'll be
that lighthouse that shines...

Bright enough to lead the blind!

At least then more will have a little peace inside...

I can't sleep at a time like this. The wind
is swift and I'm in too deep...

I must keep hope alive even though chaos is all that I see.

If any should perish, I know the cause would partly be me.

This I know!

So, through this hurricane of life instead of laying
down in fright...

I'll use all the effort and faith it takes to grow...

With courage and perseverance even when
I don't know which way to go...

Arise!!

Why should I sleep at a time like this?

Stay Silent

As clear as I can make it, as faded as I can see.

As noisy as it can sound!

As often as I can sleep...

As pure as I can store...

To listen to be assured...

What's given can be afford...

What's living can be allured...

What's different can be rehearsed.

Consistent but still the first.

Religiously Intune with Earth.

I get it I see what works.

The limit is still at birth.

To reach it is crossing lines...

To reap it is still divine...

Impeach it, it lost its mind...

I speak it but can't define...

Unleashed it though it was mine...

Top secret, soldiers align!

Exposed to provoke a lie?

No, joker stole to provide!

THE MAKE UP OF MAN

Because of this I stay humble that is how I hope to get by...

Supposedly time will tell, but I hope it stays quiet...

Knowing facts, approving wishes pray and focus on God.

I'm no Jehovah witness but I hope to enlarge.

A flash of lightening so enlightening she's supposed to discharge.

To know is to scar...

To move is Mufasa...

The Lion King, do it proper...

They're so Hakuna Matata...

No worries! I'm in a hurry I should sue every doctor...

Though I'm a law-abiding citizen I do it and lock up!

Every season's not the same.

Let's not ruin the pasta!

I just know I got my wings by staying away from the lobsters.

Many men wish death, but I dream about dollars...

A player's club, Uncle Luke I'm not the son I'm the father!

Surprised in relief. Survived in the streets!

I honor with peace!

It's a code! Blue and someone must go.

Better know it's not a secret it's the thorn of Derrick Rose.

In the game we play to win we don't just score a couple goals.

Touch down to cause hell Boosie restored a couple souls...

Enormous glitter and gold...

You either form or get enrolled!

I swore to keep her cold she got hot for a reason...

They say nothing was the same we know it's all in the season's...

Here we are with the ingredients just keep it a secret...

Your fruits of labor are digging graves...

That's a goldmine to a demon.

Reconstruction

Sometimes we see a life we never had and
get a life we never wanted.

Give to receive, roll the dice but never fumbling...

Lucky if we hit, stutter stepping sometimes stumbling...

Pain is pleasure love is one thing we be lusting.

All or nothing so we give our all to something!

Just to feel like in the end that we did it all for nothing...

But greater is coming we've been waiting even wondering...

Manifestation should be looked at as consumption.

That's reconstruction a mindset.

All in adjusting.

When time is ticking, and things should've
been different but wasn't.

I wish it wasn't, but my misses doesn't, since she rolled
with the punches, I devote to disfunction.

I get disgusted it's a sickness that I've grown to stomach.

It means more now that I feel like I'm no longer running.

Yet I insist to re-define the true meaning of hustling.

To write ones will and find the strength to free yourself from it...

Black Lives Matter

So cold, blood in every single soul...

What's life without a way to let you go...

The way they let you choke, from your stomach to your throat.

Your soul remains a shield no enemy can approach...

I just thought I'd let you know!

I see how you're moving...

Stay solid, stay strong, keep doing what you're doing...

Stay fluent, that talk you have is enough to make an influence.

Change ruins, pain reigns but we get through it...

Don't be clueless though the times seem foolish...

Just remember where your sprouts are rooted.

I Remember

I remember the times...

Pennies, nickels, and dimes...

Scraping up change even when it was hard to find...

It's funny how history repeats itself over time...

I'm still seeking change!

Equivalent to dollar signs...

I value the pain. I take pride in the hustle...

The real strength is in my heart.

I get it from the muscle!

I remember the times it seems like nobody wants you!

Alone in the dark now my shadow wants to come through...

Essence of My Presence

Whole time thinking you air and you be water...

I need you but I don't like my father...

Wonder how I stay afloat...

I challenge my every quote!

I've found it to be the hope that I stand on...

Even when I'm tripping, I'm still the ghost you can depend on...

Essence of my presence a present you should've planned on...

It's never too late! Blessings from the heavens too great.

Connect and move weights...

If you wait you start a new fate...

Don't be 2 faced, mask off! Strap up your shoelace...

True story Hershey kisses might just give you tooth aches...

It's Time to Shine!

I let you know what I'm doing before I do it... So, later
when it's done, I don't have to try to prove it....

Can't say you never knew it, we spoke fluent! You got the
message I sent. Might as well just say I grew it...

Though I must admit I felt I had to act foolish. Real rude
often aggressive. My passion was never fruitless...

I was just always taught I had to get to it. Sadly, the
truth is maybe that I really felt youth less...

Robbed of my childhood days that explains
for my childhood ways!

Am I allowed to say!

I'm creative and fully able to freestyle my ways...

Re-align my mind. Whenever It's time to shine...

Get your shine on!

Get your shine on!

I remember the times that was my song...

I don't Need No Introduction

I understand value has nothing to do with price.

You get what you paid for does it complete your life?

If you still feel lost, or you still feel cold.

Your net worth might need to network
and get right with your soul!

You must know when to go and be sure where you stay...

Re-affirm what you stand for; believe and trust if you pray!

I don't need no introduction because once I pressed play.

I was granted access the way was already paved!

The Gift That Keeps Giving

Driven by my purpose...

Passionate for change so I never feel worthless...

If I own it, I deserve it!

If I have it, I obtained it by consistent hard work and...

I struggled fighting battles every day I'm never perfect!

I speak the truth with compassion and discernment.

I'm worth a million plus though I have yet to earn it!

Never stop learning I'm a student of life...

When I finally reach my goals just know I paid that price...

I'm on a mission

If I'm missing, being distant, don't take it the hard way...

I'm a man with a vision...

Deep Conversation

Have that peace have that ease.

Have that stride have that smile.

Have that talk have those smarts.

Live for you have that style.

Don't confuse what you see.

Don't mis-announce how you feel.

Always believe in yourself.

Sometimes help isn't near.

Have that faith, keep that safe!

Keep that doubt in its place.

Keep that glow, keep that shine!

Keep your word every time.

Stay alive, well, and healthy...

Stay out of the way!

Hustle, grind, persevere, excel...

Be thankful for a new day.

A king is a friend to serving.

A queen is delicate like a ring.

Or a diamond, even gold!

After the pressure, through the mold.

Through it all it's best to obtain purity and self-control...

Be selfless though, selfish enough to not accept being broke!

Humble at most.

Selective with what you stomach the most.

Or even take in. Boast about a break-through not a break in.

Keep your mind enlightened don't let it stay dim.

A simple spark is all it takes to start the engine...!

Never race, just pace...

On that mission you embrace!

Let your ambitions stay genuine.

Opportunities, limitless.

Organize like businesses.

Realize all witnesses don't recognize what they're witnessing!

The criticism don't even consider it.

Take heed to the hate but focus more on who's listening...!

What Do You Have? What Do You Really Want?

I started off with everything and everybody
that I cherished the most...

Now all that I'm left with is nothing but hope!

It was a game of spin the bottle until a heart got broke...

Unfortunately, I became the center of all my jokes.

The same thing that makes you laugh will
make you cry that's true!

But those same tears are what will make a heart brand new.

I accept it! The hard part is moving on it's my
responsibility not to forget it.

The pain and the sorrow could easily reappear tomorrow...

So, as a reminder I'll just keep it up front.

But it never gets in the way of the life that I really want...

In Conclusion

If you don't know what it means to have visions and dreams you desire to come true... Then what is it in life that you pursue? How are you living if you have no purpose? Where's the hope of reaching your fullest potential because you're more than worth it. Life is hard but it gets better... I'm almost certain, it's easier to reach the top when you're under the most pressure. It's motivation! Everything isn't always what it seems. But hold on to your visions and dreams! They are inspiration. Everyone wants a perfect world the key is how you create it. Your heart is the source of each aspiration. Is it a dream, a nightmare, or a portrait that was well painted? What you believe is enough motivation!

Made in the USA
Middletown, DE
15 August 2021